3/16

Peeps-a-licious!

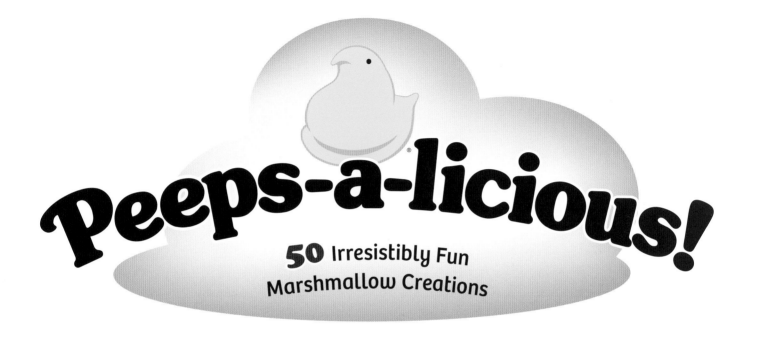

Peeps-a-licious!

50 Irresistibly Fun
Marshmallow Creations

Race Point
PUBLISHING

Quarto is the authority on a wide range of topics.
Quarto educates, entertains and enriches the lives of our readers—
enthusiasts and lovers of hands-on living.
www.quartoknows.com

First published in the United States of America in 2016 by Race Point Publishing, a member of Quarto Publishing Group USA Inc.
142 West 36th Street, 4th Floor
New York, New York 10018
www.quartoknows.com

10 9 8 7 6 5 4 3 2 1

ISBN 978-1-63106-200-1

Editorial Director: Jeannine Dillon
Managing Editor: Erin Canning
Project Editor: Jason Chappell
Interior Design: Melissa Gerber
Cover Design: Jacqui Caulton

Printed in China

CONTENTS

PEEPS® for Every Season!

One of the best things about PEEPS® is that they're available for every season. So if you want to make a PEEPS® treat for your sweetheart on Valentine's Day or for your kids on Halloween, we've got a PEEPS® for that! To make it easy, we've labeled each recipe in this book with a little PEEPS® icon (see below) to identify the season that your favorite PEEPS® is available. The PEEPS® Brand is always innovating and coming up with new, fun flavors and sometimes flavors are retired. Feel free to Express Your PEEPSONALITY® and substitute your favorite PEEPS® variety in any of these recipes. Happy baking!

 VALENTINE'S DAY

PEEPS® Strawberry Crème Chicks Dipped in Chocolate

PEEPS® Cherries Dripped and Drizzled in Chocolate

PEEPS® Vanilla Crème Hearts

PEEPS® Strawberry Crème Hearts

 EASTER

PEEPS® Marshmallow Chicks

PEEPS® Marshmallow Bunnies

PEEPS® Chocolate Mousse Chicks Dipped in Milk Chocolate

PEEPS® Marshmallow Chicks Dipped in Milk Chocolate

SUMMER

PEEPS® Patriotic Vanilla Crème Chicks

PEEPS® Sweet Lemonade Chicks

PEEPS® Party Cake Chicks

PEEPS® Sour Watermelon Chicks

PEEPS® Blue Raspberry Chicks

HALLOWEEN

PEEPS® Marshmallow Tombstones

PEEPS® Marshmallow Pumpkins

PEEPS® Marshmallow Ghosts

PEEPS® Chocolate Mousse Cats

PEEPS® Orange Chicks Dipped
in Milk Chocolate

CHRISTMAS

PEEPS® Candy Cane Chicks

PEEPS® Candy Cane Chicks
Dipped in Chocolate

PEEPS® Red Velvet Chicks
Dipped in Cream Fudge

PEEPS® Hot Cocoa & Cream Chicks
Dipped in White Fudge

PEEPS® Sugar Cookie Chicks
Dipped in Milk Chocolate

PEEPS® Chocolate Mousse Reindeer

PEEPS® Gingerbread Men

PEEPS® Marshmallow Snowmen

PEEPS® Christmas Trees

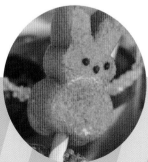

PEEPS® COOKIES AND BARS

PEEPS® Double Chocolate Cookie Sandwiches

Contributed by Sally's Baking Addiction

MAKES 8 COOKIE SANDWICHES

Ingredients

½ cup unsalted butter, softened to room temperature

½ cup granulated white sugar

½ cup light brown sugar, packed

1 large egg, at room temperature

1 teaspoon vanilla extract

1 cup all-purpose flour

½ cup plus 2 tablespoons unsweetened cocoa powder

1 teaspoon baking soda

⅛ teaspoon salt

2 tablespoons milk

1¼ cups semisweet chocolate chips

16 PEEPS® Marshmallow Bunnies, assorted colors

Directions

1 In a large bowl, beat the butter on high speed with a handheld or stand mixer fitted with a paddle attachment, until smooth and creamy, about 1 minute. Add the white and brown sugars and beat on high speed until creamed. Beat in the egg and vanilla extract. Scrape down the sides of the bowl as needed.

2 In a medium bowl, combine the flour, cocoa powder, baking soda, and salt. With the mixer on low, slowly add to the wet ingredients. Beat in the milk on high speed, then the chocolate chips on low speed. The dough will be thick and very sticky. Cover the cookie dough with plastic wrap or foil and chill for at least 2 hours and up to 36 hours.

3 Preheat oven to 350°F. Line 2 large baking sheets with parchment paper or silicone baking mats. Set aside.

4 Remove the dough from the refrigerator. Take 2 tablespoons of chilled dough, roll into a ball, and place on the cookie sheet. Repeat with remaining dough. Bake for 11–12 minutes. Cookies will appear undone and very soft. Remove from the oven and allow to cool on the baking sheets for at least 5 minutes before transferring to a wire rack to cool completely.

5 Once completely cool, place the cookies in the refrigerator for at least 30 minutes. You need cold cookies to make the sandwiches. Arrange 2 PEEPS® Bunnies on half of the cold cookies. Microwave, one by one, for 8–12 seconds until the Bunnies begin to puff up, depending on your microwave wattage. Do not microwave for any longer than that or your cookie will fall apart and be too fragile to pick up.

6 Place the remaining cookies on top of the melted PEEPS® Bunnies and press down to create sandwiches.

PEEPS® Funfetti Cookie Pie

Contributed by Love from the Oven

MAKES 8-16 SLICES

Ingredients

1 (16.5-ounce) roll refrigerated sugar cookie dough (you can also use chocolate chip or peanut butter cookie dough)

1 cup white chocolate chips, divided

½ cup rainbow sprinkles, divided

10 PEEPS® Marshmallow Bunnies, any color

1 (16-ounce) container vanilla frosting, or flavor of choice

Directions

1 Preheat oven to 325°F.

2 Break up cookie dough and place in a large bowl. Add ½ cup white chocolate chips and ¼ cup rainbow sprinkles to the dough. Combine until well mixed. (Since dough will be thick, this is easiest done by hand.)

3 Lightly press dough into an ungreased 12- or 13-inch pizza pan, covering entire pan.

4 Bake for 15–20 minutes, or until lightly browned.

5 Remove cookie pie from pan and immediately sprinkle remaining white chocolate chips and rainbow sprinkles over the top. Allow to cool completely, at least 1 hour.

6 Pipe frosting around outside edge of cookie. Place a dollop of frosting on the back of each PEEPS® Bunny and arrange Bunnies in a circle around the center of the cookie.

7 To serve, cut into 8–16 slices.

Red Velvet PEEPS® Swirl Brownies

Contributed by Kirbie's Cravings

Ingredients

½ cup semisweet chocolate chips

½ cup unsalted butter

1 cup granulated white sugar

¾ cup all-purpose flour

¼ cup unsweetened cocoa powder

1 large egg

6 PEEPS® Red Velvet Chicks Dipped in Cream Fudge, roughly chopped into fourths

Directions

1 Preheat oven to 350°F. Line an 8 x 8-inch pan with parchment paper.

2 In a small microwave-safe bowl, add chocolate chips. Heat in microwave for 30 seconds and then stir with a spatula. Heat an additional 30 seconds and stir again. After the second 30-second interval the chocolate should be completely melted and smooth. If it isn't, heat for an additional 15–30 seconds, being careful not to burn your chocolate.

3 In the bowl of a stand mixer, cream butter and sugar on high speed until light and fluffy. Add in melted chocolate, flour, cocoa powder, and egg. Mix ingredients on low speed until smooth batter forms. The batter should be very thick.

4 Scatter half of the chopped PEEPS® Chicks on the bottom of the pan. Pour brownie batter into pan, over the PEEPS®. Using a spatula, spread the batter evenly across entire pan. Gently press remaining pieces of PEEPS® Chicks halfway into the batter, forming large "S" patterns.

5 Bake for about 25–28 minutes, or until knife inserted into the brownie portion comes out clean or with only a few crumbs clinging. Let cool for about 30–60 minutes before cutting and serving.

PEEPS®-Stuffed Chocolate Chip Cookies

Contributed by Kirbie's Cravings

MAKES 12 COOKIES

Ingredients

½ cup unsalted butter, at room temperature

⅔ cup granulated white sugar

½ cup light brown sugar, packed

1 large egg

1 teaspoon vanilla extract

2 cups all-purpose flour

1 teaspoon baking soda

1/16 teaspoon salt

1 cup semisweet chocolate chips

6 PEEPS® Chocolate Mousse Chicks Dipped in Milk Chocolate

Directions

1 Preheat oven to 350°F. Line 2 large baking sheets with parchment paper or silicone baking mats.

2 In the bowl of a stand mixer, cream butter and white and brown sugars until fluffy. Add in egg and vanilla extract and mix until batter is smooth.

3 Add in flour, baking soda, and salt and mix on lowest speed until smooth dough forms. Stir in chocolate chips.

4 Using a sharp knife, cut PEEPS® Chicks into 2 pieces, head and body.

5 Using a 1½-tablespoon cookie scoop, scoop out a ball of dough and gently flatten into a disc. Place a PEEPS® Chick half in the middle of the disc. Scoop out another ball of dough with your cookie scoop and place on top of the PEEPS®. Smooth the dough over the PEEPS® until it is completely sealed inside the dough ball. Repeat with the remaining dough. You should have enough to make 12 cookies.

6 Space stuffed cookie dough balls at least 2 inches apart on baking sheets.

7 Bake for about 15–18 minutes, or until cookies are golden brown around the edges and completely cooked. Let cookies cool before eating.

PEEPS® Butterscotch Nests

Contributed by Making Time for Mommy

MAKES 15-20 NESTS

Ingredients

1 (11-ounce) package butterscotch morsels

½ cup smooth peanut butter

1½ packages (18 ounces) crispy chow mein noodles

15–20 PEEPS® Marshmallow Chicks, assorted colors

1–2 packages JUST BORN® Brand Jelly Beans, or your favorite variety (you just need white jelly beans)

Directions

1. Melt butterscotch morsels in a microwave-safe bowl in microwave for 30 seconds on high power, then stir. Continue melting for 10-second intervals, stirring after each one, until smooth.

2. Stir peanut butter into melted butterscotch and thoroughly combine.

3. Place crispy chow mein noodles into a large bowl and add butterscotch/peanut butter mixture. Combine until all noodles are coated.

4. Drop a tablespoon of chow mein mixture onto a baking sheet or plate lined with wax paper. Make an indent in the middle of the mixture to form a nest shape. Repeat with remaining mixture.

5. Refrigerate until nests harden, about 30–60 minutes.

6. To finish the nests, add 3–5 jelly beans in the center of each nest and top with a PEEPS® Chick.

PEEPS® S'mores Brownies

Contributed by Love from the Oven

MAKES 16 SERVINGS

Ingredients

Crust

1½ cups graham cracker crumbs

6 tablespoons butter, melted

2 tablespoons granulated white sugar

¼ teaspoons salt

Brownies

1 (18.4-ounce) box brownie mix and ingredients called for on the package

Topping

16 PEEPS® Marshmallow Bunnies, assorted colors, coarsely chopped into ½-inch pieces

½ cup semisweet chocolate chips

16 PEEPS® Marshmallow Bunnies, for garnish (optional)

Directions

1 Preheat oven to 325°F. Line an 8 x 8-inch pan with parchment paper or foil.

2 To make the crust, combine graham cracker crumbs, butter, sugar, and salt in a medium bowl. Mix until all ingredients start to stick together. Pour crumbs into prepared pan and firmly press mixture into pan. Bake for 20 minutes and set aside.

3 While crumb mixture is baking, prepare brownie mix according to package directions. After crumb mixture is done baking, adjust oven temperature to match the temperature called for on brownie mix instructions.

4 Pour brownie batter over crumb mixture. Work carefully as the pan will be hot. Bake in oven for time listed on brownie instructions.

5 Remove from oven and immediately top brownies with chopped PEEPS® Bunnies. Sprinkle chocolate chips over Bunnies.

6 Turn the oven to broil and place pan in oven. Broil for approximately 1 minute, or until PEEPS® start to melt and lightly brown. Make sure to watch the entire time, as the PEEPS® can melt and brown very quickly under the broiler.

7 Remove from the oven and allow to cool slightly, about 10 minutes, prior to serving. Slice into 16 pieces. Tip: For easier cutting, spray a knife with nonstick cooking spray prior to slicing.

8 If desired, top each piece with an additional PEEPS® Bunny for garnish.

PEEPS® Sugar Cookies

Contributed by Making Time for Mommy

MAKES ABOUT 48 COOKIES

Ingredients

1 cup or 2 sticks unsalted butter, at room temperature

1 cup granulated white sugar

1½ teaspoons vanilla extract

1 egg, lightly beaten

2 cups all-purpose flour

½ teaspoon cream of tartar

½ teaspoon baking powder

Wax paper

Sprinkles

48 PEEPS® Marshmallow Chicks, assorted colors

Directions

1 Cream together butter and sugar in large bowl. Add in vanilla extract and egg, and combine well.

2 Mix in flour, cream of tartar, and baking powder, and stir until dough is well-combined.

3 Cut dough into 4 equal pieces.

4 Place a dough piece on a sheet of 8 x 11-inch wax paper. Wrap it in the wax paper and roll into a small log shape.

5 Pour sprinkles onto a plate. Open up the wax paper, remove the dough log, and roll the dough in the sprinkles until covered.

6 Rewrap dough in the wax paper and refrigerate for 1 hour. Repeat Steps 4–6 with the 3 remaining pieces of dough.

7 Once chilled, remove dough from wax paper and slice each log into ½-inch-thick rounds. Place on a nonstick baking sheet.

8 Preheat oven to 375°F and bake cookies for 6–8 minutes.

9 After 6–8 minutes, take the cookies out of oven. Place a PEEPS® Chick on top of each cookie while the cookies are warm and soft. Put cookies back in oven for another 2 minutes.

10 Let cool to room temperature and store in an airtight container.

24

PEEPS® Peek-a-Boo S'mores Fudge

Contributed by Kirbie's Cravings

Ingredients

3 cups semisweet chocolate chips

1 (14-ounce) can sweetened condensed milk

1½ sheets graham crackers, crushed

20 PEEPS® Marshmallow Bunnies, assorted colors

Directions

1 In a large microwave-safe bowl, combine chocolate chips and condensed milk. Heat in the microwave for 30 seconds and then stir. Heat again for an additional 30 seconds and stir again. After the second interval, the chocolate should be completely melted and smooth. If it isn't, heat for an additional 15–30 seconds, being careful not to overheat or burn the chocolate.

2 Line a 9 x 9-inch baking pan with parchment paper. Sprinkle half the graham crackers across the pan. Pour fudge mixture on top. (The fudge will be quite thick and you can smooth out the surface with your hands or a spatula.)

3 Using a sharp knife, remove the Bunny heads from the bodies and set them aside. (Discard or eat the bodies!)

4 Place Bunny heads so it looks like they're peeking out from the surface of the fudge. Take remaining graham cracker pieces and place them around Bunnies, gently pressing both the cracker and marshmallow into the fudge to secure them.

5 Place fudge in the refrigerator to solidify for several hours or overnight.

6 Remove fudge from the refrigerator and use a sharp knife to slice it into small squares. Store any uneaten pieces in an airtight container in the refrigerator for up to 1 week.

PEEPS® Red Velvet Whoopie Pies

Contributed by Chef Melanie Underwood

MAKES 12 SMALL WHOOPIE PIES

Ingredients

Whoopie Pies

1½ cups all-purpose flour

3 tablespoons unsweetened cocoa powder

½ teaspoon baking powder

¼ teaspoon baking soda

¼ teaspoon salt

½ cup or 1 stick unsalted butter, at room temperature

2 PEEPS® Red Velvet Chicks Dipped in Cream Fudge, finely chopped

½ cup granulated white sugar

¼ cup light brown sugar, packed

1 egg

1 teaspoon vanilla extract

2 teaspoons red food coloring

½ cup buttermilk

Cream Cheese Filling

6 PEEPS® Red Velvet Chicks Dipped in Cream Fudge

8 ounces cream cheese, at room temperature

½ cup or 1 stick unsalted butter, at room temperature

1 cup confectioners' sugar

Directions

1 Preheat oven to 350°F. Line a baking sheet with parchment paper.

2 To make the whoopie pies, whisk together the flour, cocoa powder, baking powder, baking soda, and salt in a medium bowl, and set aside.

3 In the bowl of a stand mixer using the paddle attachment, cream together the butter, chopped PEEPS®, and white and brown sugars on medium speed until light and fluffy, about 7–8 minutes.

4 Add the egg and mix about 1 minute until completely combined.

5 Add the vanilla extract and food coloring, and mix until just blended.

6 Turn the mixer off and add half of the flour mixture and mix on low until just incorporated. While mixer is still on low, slowly pour in the buttermilk. Turn off the mixer and scrape down the sides of the bowl. Add the remaining flour mixture and mix on low just until combined.

7 Using a small ice cream scoop, scoop 24 rounds of the batter and place on prepared baking sheet about 2 inches apart.

8 Bake for about 10 minutes, or until the whoopie pies spring back when touched. Remove from the oven and allow to cool completely before filling, about 30 minutes.

9 To make the cream cheese filling, add the PEEPS® Chicks to the bowl of a food processor and pulse about 1 minute, or until the PEEPS® are finely ground. Add in the cream cheese and butter and continue mixing until the mixture is light and smooth, about 30 seconds. Add in the confectioners' sugar and mix until combined, another 30 seconds.

10 To assemble, spread the filling onto the flat side of one whoopie pie using an offset spatula. Top with another whoopie pie.

11 Store wrapped tightly in plastic wrap in the refrigerator up to 5 days.

The PEEPS®
Crispy Rice Treat

Contributed by Cute As a Fox

Ingredients

3 tablespoons margarine

36 PEEPS® Marshmallow Bunnies or 40 PEEPS® Marshmallow Chicks, yellow*

6 cups crispy rice cereal

Nonstick cooking spray

*Make your crispy rice treats match the occasion by using different-colored marshmallow PEEPS®—pink PEEPS® will result in pink treats and so on.

Directions

1. In a 5-quart or larger saucepan, heat the margarine over low heat. When the margarine has completely melted, add the PEEPS® Bunnies or Chicks. Heat PEEPS® until completely melted, stirring occasionally. Remove from heat.

2. Stir in the crispy rice cereal until the cereal is completely coated in marshmallow. Spray a 9 x 13-inch baking pan with nonstick cooking spray. Turn the treats out into the pan and press down into an even layer with a greased spatula or greased hands. Let the treats cool approximately 30 minutes.

3. To serve, cut into 2 x 2-inch squares (see page 2 for a photo of the finished product).

PEEPS® CAKES AND CUPCAKES

PEEPS® Party Cupcake Cones

Contributed by Love from the Oven

Ingredients

Cupcake Cones

24 flat-bottom ice cream cones

1 (15.25-ounce) box cake mix and ingredients called for on the package, flavor of choice

Frosting

2 cups or 4 sticks butter, softened

⅓ cup heavy whipping cream

1 tablespoon vanilla extract

8 cups confectioners' sugar

Garnish

24 PEEPS® Marshmallow Chicks, assorted colors

Rainbow sprinkles

Directions

1 Preheat oven to 350°F.

2 Stand ice cream cones in muffin pans.

3 To make the cupcakes, prepare cake mix according to package directions. Fill each ice cream cone half full of cake batter.

4 Bake for approximately 21–24 minutes, or until a toothpick inserted into the top of cake comes out clean. Remove from oven and allow to cool completely, at least 20 minutes.

5 While cones are cooling, make the frosting. Beat butter with a mixer in a large bowl until light and fluffy, about 2 minutes. Add cream and vanilla extract and beat until well combined. Slowly add in confectioners' sugar and beat until mixed. Once mixed, beat for an additional 2 minutes on medium. Frosting should have a thick consistency. If it's too runny, add more confectioners' sugar, 1 tablespoon at a time, until desired consistency is reached.

6 Spoon frosting into a large zip-top bag. Clip one corner end off, about ½ inch, or use a piping bag and pipe frosting onto the top of cupcake cones. A simple swirl will recreate the look of soft serve ice cream. Top each cupcake cone with a PEEPS® Chick and sprinkles.

PEEPS® for Peace Cake

Contributed by A Sweet and Savory Life

MAKES 12 SERVINGS

Ingredients

Cake

Nonstick cooking spray for greasing

2½ cups cake flour, sifted, plus additional for dusting

1½ teaspoons baking powder

½ teaspoon baking soda

½ teaspoon salt

1⅓ cups granulated white sugar

½ cup or 1 stick unsalted butter, softened

2 large eggs

1 cup lowfat buttermilk

1 tablespoon vanilla extract

Frosting

1½ cups or 3 sticks unsalted butter at room temperature

4 cups confectioners' sugar, sifted

2 teaspoons vanilla extract

2 tablespoons heavy cream

Red, yellow, green, and blue liquid food coloring

9 PEEPS® Marshmallow Chicks, assorted colors

Directions

1 Preheat oven to 350°F. Coat two 9-inch cake pans with nonstick cooking spray and dust lightly with flour.

2 To make the cake, combine the flour, baking powder, baking soda, and salt in a medium bowl. Set aside.

3 In a large bowl, beat the sugar and butter with an electric mixer at medium speed until well blended, about 4 minutes. Add the eggs and beat on medium speed until the mixture is light and fluffy, stopping occasionally to scrape down the sides of the bowl, another 4 minutes.

4 In a small bowl, combine the buttermilk and vanilla extract. With the mixer on low, beat the flour mixture into the buttermilk mixture and then into the butter mixture alternately in 2 additions.

5 Divide the batter evenly between the prepared pans and tap each lightly on the counter a few times to remove any air bubbles from the batter. Bake until a toothpick inserted into the center of each cake comes out clean, about 25–26 minutes. Remove from the oven and cool in the pans for about 10 minutes. Remove from the pans and cool layers completely on wire racks.

37

6 To make the frosting, beat butter in a large bowl with an electric mixer until softened. Add the confectioners' sugar and beat until smooth and fluffy. Add the vanilla extract and cream and beat again until smooth.

7 Remove 1 cup frosting and divide it evenly among 4 small bowls to make the colored frosting. Add 1 drop of yellow food coloring to the first bowl; 1 drop of red to the second; 1 drop of green to the third; and about half a drop each of red and blue to the fourth bowl. Transfer each color to its own sandwich-size plastic bag. (May be made ahead and refrigerated for up to 1 week.)

8 Take one of the cakes and invert on a serving dish so the flat side faces up. Spread with a layer of uncolored frosting and top with the second cake layer, again with the flat side facing up. Starting with the sides, use the uncolored frosting to cover the entire outside. Refrigerate at least 1 hour before decorating.

9 To decorate the cake, squeeze each colored frosting to a bottom corner of its plastic bag and snip the end to form a tiny pinhole from which you will pipe the decoration. To make the "psychedelic swirl" on the side of the cake, start by piping one long thin swirl and smear the swirl with a dampened fingertip. Continue with the other colors until the sides of the cake are covered in the 4 colors.

10 Use the remaining colored frosting to draw a peace sign on the top of the cake and to draw peace necklaces on the PEEPS®. Place the Chicks decoratively on the cake.

Marshmallow-Filled PEEPS® Cupcakes

Contributed by Sally's Baking Addiction

MAKES 18 CUPCAKES

Ingredients

Cupcakes

2 cups cake flour

1¾ teaspoons baking powder

½ teaspoon salt

3 large eggs, at room temperature and separated

½ cup unsalted butter, softened to room temperature

1 tablespoon vanilla extract

1½ cups granulated white sugar

⅔ cup whole milk, at room temperature

Marshmallow Frosting and Topping

1 cup or 2 sticks unsalted butter, softened to room temperature

1 cup marshmallow creme

1½ teaspoons vanilla extract

¼ cup heavy cream

3 cups confectioners' sugar

¼ teaspoon salt, plus more to taste

Food coloring in color of your choice (optional)

18 PEEPS® Marshmallow Chicks, assorted colors

Directions

1. Preheat oven to 350°F. Line a 12-count muffin pan with cupcake liners. (This recipe makes 18 cupcakes, so you will have 6 cupcakes to bake in a second batch.)

2. To make the cupcakes, sift the flour, baking powder, and ½ teaspoon salt together in a large bowl. Set aside.

3. With a handheld or stand mixer fitted with a whisk attachment, beat the egg whites on high speed in a medium bowl until soft peaks form, about 2–3 minutes. Set aside.

4. With a handheld or stand mixer fitted with a paddle attachment, beat the butter on high speed in a large bowl until smooth and creamy, about 1 minute. Add the sugar and beat on high speed for 3–4 minutes, until creamed. Scrape down the sides and up the bottom of the bowl with a rubber spatula as needed.

39

5 Add the egg yolks and vanilla extract. Beat on medium-high speed until combined. Scrape the bowl again as needed. With the mixer on low speed, add the dry ingredients in 3 additions, alternating with the milk and mixing after each addition until just incorporated. Do not overmix.

6 Using a rubber spatula, gently fold in the egg whites until combined. The batter will be slightly thick.

7 Spoon batter into cupcake liners, filling halfway. Bake for 22–24 minutes or until the tops of the cupcakes spring back when gently touched and a toothpick inserted in the center comes out clean. Remove from the oven and allow to cool in the pan for 5 minutes, then transfer to a rack to cool completely.

8 To make the frosting, beat the butter, marshmallow creme, vanilla extract, and cream in a large bowl with a handheld or stand mixer fitted with a whisk attachment on medium speed until smooth and creamy. Add the confectioners' sugar and ¼ teaspoon salt slowly with the mixer running on low, then increase the speed to high and beat for 1 minute. Taste. Add a pinch more salt if desired. If using food coloring to create colored frosting, beat in the food coloring to reach your desired color. Refrigerate the frosting until ready to use.

9 To assemble the cupcakes, cut a hole in the center of each cupcake using a sharp knife to create a little pocket about ¾ inch deep. Place 1 spoonful (a little more than 1 teaspoon) of marshmallow filling inside and top with the piece of cupcake you removed to seal. Frost the cupcakes with remaining frosting. Top with a PEEPS® Chick.

PEEPS® Mini Baked Donuts

Contributed by Kirbie's Cravings

MAKES 24 MINI DONUTS

Ingredients

Donuts

¾ cup granulated white sugar

1 large egg

1½ cups all-purpose flour

2 teaspoons baking power

¼ teaspoon salt

¼ teaspoon ground nutmeg

¼ cup vegetable oil, plus additional for greasing

¾ cup fat free milk

1 teaspoon vanilla extract

8 PEEPS® Marshmallow Chicks, roughly chopped into pieces the size of chocolate chips

Glaze

16 PEEPS® Marshmallow Chicks (in either one color or assorted colors)

2 cups confectioners' sugar

2 tablespoons water

Directions

1 Preheat oven to 350°F. Grease 2 mini donut pans by brushing donut molds with oil.

2 To make the donuts, whisk together sugar and egg in a large bowl. Add in remaining ingredients except chopped PEEPS®, and whisk until batter is smooth. Stir in PEEPS®.

3 Spoon batter about two-thirds full into prepared pans. Bake for about 10 minutes, or until knife inserted into donut comes out clean.

4 Let donuts cool in pans for about 30 minutes. Once cooled, use a small spatula to help release donuts.

5 To make the glaze, combine all ingredients in a small saucepan. Over medium heat, stir constantly until PEEPS® Chicks melt and glaze becomes uniform, then reduce heat to low. Working quickly, spoon the glaze over the donuts. You do not want the glaze in the saucepan to cool, otherwise it will harden. If you'd like to make an assortment of colored glazes, melt 4 PEEPS® Chicks of a single color with ½ cup confectioners' sugar and ½ teaspoon water. This is enough glaze for 6 mini donuts.

6 For an extra decoration option, you can also sprinkle the excess sparkling sanding sugar inside the PEEPS® packaging over the glazed donuts before the glaze solidifies. Let glaze cool and harden before serving donuts.

No-Bake Lemon PEEPS® Cake

Contributed by Love from the Oven

MAKES 24 SERVINGS

Ingredients

1 (11-ounce) package vanilla wafers

½ cup or 1 stick butter, melted

1 (8-ounce) package (not tub) cream cheese, softened

¼ cup granulated white sugar

2 tablespoons 2% milk

1½ (12-ounce) containers whipped topping (such as Cool Whip)

2 (3.4-ounce) packages lemon-flavored instant pudding (or flavor of your choice)

3¼ cups 2% milk

Yellow sprinkles (optional)

30 PEEPS® Marshmallow Chicks, yellow (or try PEEPS® Sweet Lemonade Chicks)

Directions

1 In a food processor, process vanilla wafers into crumbs. Add melted butter and pulse until all of vanilla wafer crumbs are moistened.

2 Press crumb mixture into the bottom of a 13 x 9-inch pan.

3 Beat cream cheese with an electric mixer until light and fluffy, about 2 minutes. Add in sugar and 2 tablespoons milk and mix until well combined. Stir in 1¼ cups whipped topping. Spoon mixture on top of crumb mixture and spread to cover.

4 In a medium bowl, beat pudding and 3¼ cups milk with a whisk for 2 minutes. Pour mixture over the cream cheese layer. Place in the refrigerator for 15 minutes.

5 Cut 6 PEEPS® Chicks into small pieces, approximately ¼–⅓ inches in diameter.

6 In a large bowl, combine the chopped PEEPS® Chicks with remaining whipped topping. Remove cake from the refrigerator and spread whipped topping mixture over pudding mixture. Return to refrigerator and chill for at least 4 hours.

7 To serve, slice into 24 pieces. Top each piece with yellow sprinkles, if desired, and a PEEPS® Chick. Store in refrigerator.

 44

PEEPS® Bunny Patch Cake

Contributed by Just Born

MAKES 1 (9-INCH) CAKE

Ingredients

1 (15.25-ounce) box cake mix and ingredients called for on the package, flavor of choice

1 (16-ounce) container chocolate frosting, or your homemade recipe

Approximately 30 PEEPS® Marshmallow Bunnies, assorted colors

3 chocolate sugar wafer cookies

1 green MIKE AND IKE® Brand candy

3 orange MIKE AND IKE® Brand candies

Decorative picket fencing (available at craft stores; optional)

5–6 toothpicks

Directions

1 Preheat oven to 350°F.

2 Prepare and bake cake according to package instructions in a 9-inch round cake pan. Let the cake cool to room temperature.

3 Frost cake with chocolate frosting, reserving 1 tablespoon of frosting.

4 Attach approximately 24 PEEPS® Bunnies, alternating colors and touching one another, to the side of the cake, wrapping around the entire cake.

5 For the top, create a small planter box using the chocolate sugar wafer cookies. Cut 1 wafer cookie into thirds. Use the 2 whole wafer cookies as the front and back parts of the planter and 2 of the 3 pieces of the third cookie as the planter sides. Crush the remaining cookie piece to fill the planter, then top with reserved tablespoon of frosting.

6 Cut the green MIKE AND IKE® candy into 3 pieces and top as carrot tops to the 3 orange candies that will be the carrots. Adhere to the orange candies using the cut, sticky sides.

7 Plant the MIKE AND IKE® carrots in the planter.

8 Insert toothpicks halfway into the bottoms of remaining Bunnies, then insert into the top of the cake.

9 Add picket fencing to top of cake, if desired.

47

PEEPS® Ombré Bunny Cupcakes

Contributed by Cute As a Fox

Ingredients

Ombré Cupcakes

1 (15.25-ounce) box white cake mix and ingredients called for on the package

Pink gel food coloring

Buttercream Frosting

½ cup or 1 stick butter, softened

1½ teaspoons clear vanilla extract

4–6 tablespoons milk

4–4½ cups confectioners' sugar

Pink or red food coloring

¼ cup pink sanding sugar

Ombré PEEPS® Bunnies

18 PEEPS® Marshmallow Bunnies, pink

Pink food color spray

Directions

1 Preheat oven to 350°F.

2 To make the cupcakes, mix the white cake mix according to the package instructions. (Feel free to substitute your favorite from-scratch recipe for white cake if you like.)

3 Divide the batter equally into three 3-cup or larger bowls. Put one bowl aside. Add pink gel coloring to the second bowl to achieve a light pink color. Add even more gel coloring to the third bowl to get a deep pink color.

4 Add a generous tablespoon of dark pink, light pink, and white batter, in layers, to each cupcake liner. Bake at 350°F for 18–24 minutes, or until a toothpick comes out clean. Allow the cupcakes to cool completely, about 1 hour.

5 To make the frosting, in a large bowl, beat butter until creamy with a hand mixer or stand mixer. Beat in vanilla extract. Add confectioners' sugar, 1 cup at a time, and beat until incorporated. When frosting becomes too dry, add 1 tablespoon milk. Alternate between adding milk and sugar until 4 tablespoons milk and 4 cups confectioners' sugar have been added. If consistency needs to be adjusted, use additional confectioners' sugar to thicken and milk to thin. Use food coloring to reach desired pink tint.

6 Frost each cooled cupcake with buttercream frosting. Sprinkle lightly with pink sanding sugar.

7 To make the ombré PEEPS® Bunnies, wrap the top two-thirds of each Bunny with plastic wrap. Spray the exposed third of the Bunny with pink food color spray. Spray several light coats to get a nice dark pink color. Allow the Bunnies to dry 5–10 minutes before removing the plastic wrap.

8 Quickly dip the Bunny ears into water, then pat dry with a paper towel. The combination of the water and the paper towel will begin to remove the pink color from the ears. Repeat this process a few times until you have removed the desired amount of pink. The exposed white marshmallow will be sticky, so keep that in mind when working with the PEEPS®. The middle third of the PEEPS® Bunny will stay the original shade of pink. The finished Bunny should start with a white and pink speckled look at the ears and transition to the original shade of pink, then into the dark pink color.

9 Top the frosted ombré cupcakes with the ombré PEEPS® Bunnies.

49

PEEPS® Chocolate Peppermint Cupcakes

Contributed by Love from the Oven

MAKES 24 CUPCAKES

Ingredients

Cupcakes

1 (18.25-ounce) box chocolate cake mix, such as devil's food or chocolate fudge

1 cup granulated white sugar

⅓ cup unsweetened cocoa powder (preferably dark cocoa powder)

⅔ cup all-purpose flour

1 cup water (cooled coffee can also be used)

3 eggs

1 teaspoon peppermint extract

1 cup mini chocolate chips (this is optional, but really kicks up the chocolate flavor!)

1 cup sour cream

Frosting

1 cup or 2 sticks butter, softened

4 cups confectioners' sugar

Pinch of salt

1 teaspoon peppermint extract

1 teaspoon vanilla extract

1 teaspoon heavy whipping cream (you can also use milk or half-and-half)

1 tablespoon butter

4 PEEPS® Candy Cane Chicks (not dipped in chocolate)

24 PEEPS® Candy Cane Chicks Dipped in Chocolate, for garnish

Chocolate syrup and crushed candy canes, for garnish (optional)

Directions

1. Preheat oven to 325°F. Line two 12-count cupcake pans with 24 cupcake liners.

2. To make cupcakes, combine cake mix, sugar, cocoa, and flour in a large bowl. Mix to combine. Add in water, eggs, peppermint extract, mini chocolate chips if using, and sour cream. Mix for approximately 2 minutes using an electric mixer.

3 Scoop cupcake batter into cupcake liners. Batter should fill the cupcake liners about two-thirds of the way full. Place cupcakes in oven to bake for 15–20 minutes, or until center springs back when lightly touched and a toothpick inserted into the center comes out clean. Remove from the oven and allow to cool completely on cooling racks.

4 To make the frosting, beat 1 cup (2 sticks) butter with an electric mixer in a small mixing bowl until light and fluffy. Mix in confectioners' sugar and salt, blending well. Add in peppermint extract, vanilla extract, and cream, and mix on medium for approximately 2 minutes. Set aside.

5 In a heavy medium saucepan over low heat, melt 1 tablespoon butter with 4 Candy Cane Chicks (not dipped in chocolate). Stir until PEEPS® have dissolved and combined with melted butter. Remove from heat and allow to cool for approximately 5 minutes.

6 Add PEEPS® mixture to frosting and mix with an electric mixer until well combined. If frosting is too thin, add extra confectioners' sugar, 1 tablespoon at a time, until desired consistency is reached.

7 Frost cupcakes by either piping on frosting or spreading it on with a knife. To pipe, place frosting in a large zip-top bag. Snip a ⅓-inch opening off one of the bottom corners of the bag. Gently squeeze frosting out of bag and onto cupcake while slowly rotating cupcake. Top each cupcake with a Candy Cane Chick Dipped in Chocolate.

PEEPS® Berry Crumble

Contributed by Chef Melanie Underwood

Ingredients

Filling

4 cups pitted sour cherries, coarsely chopped

⅓ cup granulated white sugar

1 tablespoon cornstarch

1 tablespoon lemon juice

Crumble

1 cup all-purpose flour

6 PEEPS® Strawberry Crème Hearts

½ cup rolled oats

2 tablespoons light brown sugar, packed

½ teaspoon cinnamon

½ cup or 1 stick unsalted butter, melted

Directions

1 Preheat oven to 350°F.

2 To make the filling, combine sour cherries, sugar, cornstarch, and lemon juice in a large bowl. Pour into an 8 x 8-inch baking dish and set aside.

3 To make the crumble, combine flour, PEEPS® Hearts, oats, brown sugar, and cinnamon in a large bowl. Stir in the melted butter until completely combined.

4 Sprinkle the crumble on top of the filling. Bake for about 30 minutes, or until the fruit is bubbly and syrupy. Remove from oven and cool slightly before serving.

PEEPS® GOURMET

PEEPS® Macarons

Contributed by That's So Michelle

MAKES 12 MACARONS

Ingredients

3 egg whites, refrigerated overnight

¼ cup granulated white sugar

1⅔ cups confectioners' sugar

1 cup almond meal

2 pastry bags

Wilton gel food coloring of choice

6 PEEPS® Marshmallow Chicks, any color, halved

Decorating sugar, colors of choice

Directions

1 Preheat oven to 280°F. Line a baking sheet with parchment paper or a silicone mat.

2 Bring egg whites to room temperature and pour into a large mixing bowl. Beat with an electric mixer until egg whites are foamy. Pour in white sugar and continue beating until egg whites are slightly stiff and hold soft peaks. You should be able to turn your bowl upside down without the egg whites falling out. Be careful not to overmix.

3 Sift confectioners' sugar and almond meal into a separate large mixing bowl (don't skip this step), then fold the almond mixture into the egg white mixture until combined. Again, do not overmix. Stir in food coloring to reach desired color.

4 Spoon all of macaron batter into a pastry bag and line the baking sheet with twenty-four 1½-inch circles of batter. Firmly yet gently slam the baking sheet onto the counter to release any air pockets in the batter.

5 Place baking sheet into the oven and bake for 10 minutes. Cookies should be set but not browned, and should have "feet" (the texturized and ridged bottom of the macaroon). Remove from the oven and let cool completely before filling.

6 For the filling, microwave half a PEEPS® Chick for 10 seconds on high power in a small microwave-safe bowl. Spoon the melted Chick onto a cookie and gently press a second cookie on top to sandwich it. Repeat to make a total of 12 cookies.

7 Roll the macarons in colored sugar. Keep in a cool place until serving.

PEEPS® Cloud Angels

Contributed by A Sweet and Savory Life

MAKES ABOUT 15 CLOUD ANGELS

Ingredients

8 large egg whites, at room temperature

½ teaspoon cream of tartar

2 cups granulated white sugar

2 teaspoons vanilla extract

15 PEEPS® Marshmallow Chicks, white

6–8 yellow spice or gum drops

Directions

1. Preheat oven to 225°F. Line 2 baking sheets with parchment paper.

2. In a large bowl, beat egg whites on medium speed with an electric mixer until foamy. Add cream of tartar and beat on medium speed until soft peaks form. Increase speed to medium high and very slowly add the sugar and then the vanilla extract. Beat to stiff peaks.

3. Working one at a time, use a soup spoon to drop a dollop of the meringue mixture onto the prepared sheet pan. Use the back of the spoon to form an indentation in the center of each dollop, approximately the length of a PEEPS® Chick. (This allows the PEEPS® to rest on a flat surface).

4. Bake the meringue clouds until they readily release from the parchment but are not browned, about 45 minutes.

5. Turn the oven off and allow the meringues to cool in the oven for 15 minutes. Remove from the oven and cool at room temperature.

6. To make the halos, cut a gum (or spice) drop across the width into very thin slices to form circles. Use the tip of a small knife to cut out the center of each slice, leaving a thin ring. Place a ring on top of each Chick's head. Gently affix the center of each ring to the underside of the Peep.

7. Place each PEEPS® Chick on a cooled cloud, allowing the gum drop to lightly affix to the meringue on the underside. Serve.

8. Store at room temperature for up to several days.

PEEPS® Rainbow Sushi

Contributed by That's So Michelle

MAKES 16 PIECES

Ingredients

6 PEEPS® crispy rice treats, divided (see page 31 for recipe)

10 PEEPS® Marshmallow Chicks, assorted colors

10 strips fruit leather (approximately 1 x 4 inches each), divided

8 (2-inch) white chocolate squares

6 PEEPS® Marshmallow Bunnies, assorted colors (you can substitute Bunnies for Chicks)

Decorating sugar, colors of choice

Directions

PEEPS® Sushi with Chicks

1 Halve 3 crispy rice treats to make 6 rectangles. Top each half with a PEEPS® Chick.

2 Using a knife, slice 6 strips fruit leather into ¾-inch-wide strips. Wrap a strip completely around one of the crispy rice halves with a PEEPS® Chick on top, securing the Chick to the square. Repeat with remaining 5 Chicks and crispy rice halves.

3 Place a PEEPS® Chick on top of 2 white chocolate squares. Repeat with remaining 3 Chicks and chocolate squares.

PEEPS® Rolls with Bunnies

1 Using a rolling pin, roll remaining 3 crispy rice treats as flat as you can without breaking them. Halve each square to make 6 rectangles.

2 Cut a PEEPS® Bunny in half horizontally. Carefully wrap the flattened crispy rice half completely around the top half (the half with ears) of the Bunny. (You can discard or eat the bottom half!)

3 Wrap a strip of fruit leather around the outside of the crispy rice. Repeat with remaining 5 Bunnies and crispy rice halves.

4 Roll the wrapped Bunnies in colored decorating sugar.

Stuffed PEEPS® Candy Surprise

Contributed by A Sweet and Savory Life

Ingredients

3 tablespoons mini chocolate chips, divided

3 tablespoons toffee bits

8 very thin pretzel sticks, broken into small pieces

2 tablespoons toasted coconut flakes

48 PEEPS® Marshmallow Chicks, assorted colors

Directions

1 In a medium saucepan over low heat, melt 2 tablespoons chocolate chips, then stir in the toffee bits, pretzels, and coconut. Stir in the remaining 1 tablespoon chocolate chips.

2 Remove from heat and let stand until hardened, about 10 minutes.

3 Using your hands, break into ¼-inch pieces.

4 Use the tip of a sharp knife to make a ½-inch-long cut in the center of the underside of one of the PEEPS® Chicks. The cut should be about ½ inch deep. Insert as much of the chocolate mixture as fits into the cut, pushing it in with your fingertip. Close the slit by pushing it together. Place on a plate.

5 Repeat with the remaining PEEPS® Chicks.

PEEPS® Crème Brûlée

Contributed by Chef Melanie Underwood

Ingredients

2 cups heavy cream

8 PEEPS® Marshmallow Bunnies, any color, halved

4 large egg yolks

1½ teaspoons vanilla extract

4 PEEPS® Marshmallow Bunnies, any color, halved vertically, for garnish

Directions

1. Preheat oven to 300°F. Combine heavy cream and 8 halved Bunnies in a medium saucepan over medium heat, stirring occasionally until PEEPS® are melted. Remove from heat and allow to slightly cool, about 5 minutes.

2. In the meantime, whisk together yolks and vanilla extract in a medium bowl. Slowly whisk PEEPS® mixture into the egg yolks until completely combined.

3. Place 4 ramekins in a baking pan, then divide the mixture evenly among the ramekins. Add enough hot water to the baking pan to come halfway up sides of ramekins. Bake until custards are set and firm to the touch, about 45–50 minutes. Remove from baking pan and let sit for 20 minutes, then place in refrigerator for at least 30 minutes before serving.

4. When ready to serve, place the 4 vertically halved PEEPS® Bunnies on a baking sheet without parchment paper. Using a butane torch, caramelize the PEEPS® Bunnies until golden brown on the exposed marshmallow side, about 20 seconds. Allow the PEEPS® to cool, about 1 minute, then place 2 PEEPS® Bunnies, caramelized side up, atop the crème brûlée in each ramekin.

PEEPS® Raspberry Marshmallow Crepes

Contributed by Just Born

MAKES 4 CREPES

Ingredients

Filling

1 teaspoon raspberry-flavored extract
(may substitute ¼ cup raspberry jam)

1 (12-ounce) container whipped topping

6 PEEPS® Marshmallow Bunnies or Chicks,
lavender, cut into ¼-inch pieces

Crepes

2 eggs

½ cup milk

½ cup water

1 cup all-purpose flour

¼ teaspoon salt

2 tablespoons butter, melted

⅓ cup granulated white sugar

½ cup confectioners' sugar, divided

4 PEEPS® Marshmallow Bunnies or Chicks,
lavender, for garnish

Directions

1 To make the filling, mix together raspberry-flavored extract and whipped topping in a medium mixing bowl until well combined.

2 Fold the PEEPS® pieces into the whipped topping mixture. Set filling aside or refrigerate until crepes are ready to fill.

3 To make the crepes, whisk the eggs in a large mixing bowl.

4 Gradually add in the milk and water, then sift in flour, stirring to combine.

5 Add the salt, butter, granulated sugar, and ¼ cup confectioners' sugar. Beat until smooth.

6 Heat a lightly oiled medium frying pan or crepe pan over medium-high heat.

7 Pour or scoop ¼ cup batter into the pan. Tilt the pan in a circular motion so that the batter coats the surface evenly. Cook for about 2 minutes, or until the bottom is light brown. Loosen with a spatula, turn, and cook the other side. Carefully slide crepe out of pan and onto a plate. Repeat for remaining 3 crepes.

8 Scoop about ½ cup filling into each crepe and roll. Top each crepe with a small amount of remaining confectioners' sugar and a Bunny or Chick, and serve immediately.

PEEPS® Reindeer Chocolate Mousse Cups

Contributed by Love from the Oven

SERVES 4

Ingredients

1 cup semisweet chocolate chips

1 tablespoon butter

6 PEEPS® Chocolate Mousse Reindeer, divided

1 (8-ounce) container whipped topping (optional)

Chocolate sprinkles (optional)

Directions

1 Combine chocolate chips, butter, and 2 PEEPS® Reindeer in a medium microwave-safe bowl.

2 Microwave on half power for 30 seconds. Remove from microwave and stir. Continue to microwave in 15-second intervals until chocolate chips, butter, and PEEPS® are melted. Stir well to combine. Mixture will be very thick. Allow mixture to cool for 5 minutes.

3 In a large bowl, combine whipped topping and melted chocolate mixture. Mix with an electric mixer on low until just combined.

4 Evenly spoon mixture into 4 individual serving dishes or cups. Refrigerate for at least 2 hours prior to serving. Top each serving with a PEEPS® Reindeer and additional whipped topping and sprinkles, if desired.

5 Store tightly covered in the refrigerator for up to 1 week.

PEEPS® Peppermint Ricotta Cheesecake

Contributed by Chef Melanie Underwood

MAKES 1 (8-INCH) CHEESECAKE

Ingredients

Crust

9 sheets graham crackers, broken in half

6 PEEPS® Marshmallow Snowmen, halved

¼ cup or ½ stick butter, melted

Cheesecake

16 ounces cream cheese

16 ounces ricotta cheese

¾ cup granulated white sugar

4 large eggs

2 teaspoons peppermint extract

8 cups water

6–8 PEEPS® Candy Cane Chicks Dipped in Chocolate, for garnish

Directions

1 Preheat oven to 325°F.

2 To make the crust, add the graham crackers and PEEPS® Snowmen to the bowl of a food processor. Pulse together until completely ground and PEEPS® are no longer visible, about 1 minute. Pour in melted butter and pulse until the crust comes together, about 30 seconds.

3 Remove from the food processor and pour into an 8-inch springform pan. Using the palm of your hand or the bottom of a glass, press the mixture firmly into the bottom of the pan. Place the pan in the freezer for 10–15 minutes, or until completely firm.

4 To make the cheesecake, place the cream cheese and ricotta in the bowl of a stand mixer. Using the paddle attachment, combine on low speed until softened, about 2 minutes, scraping down the sides of the bowl, underneath the paddle, and the paddle frequently with a rubber spatula.

5 Add the sugar and continue mixing on low speed while continuing to scrape down the sides, bottom, and paddle until there are no visible lumps. Add the eggs one at a time and mix until just combined, about 10 seconds after each egg. Stir in the peppermint extract.

71

6 Prepare the springform pan for a water bath by wrapping the bottom and sides in plastic wrap coming almost to the top of the pan and then in foil, coming almost to the top of the pan. Place the springform pan in a roasting pan.

7 Boil 8 cups water. Once boiled, remove from heat.

8 Pour the batter over the crust. Place the roasting pan in the oven and pour the almost-boiling water into the roasting pan. The water should come almost halfway up the side of the springform pan. Bake about 90 minutes, until the cheesecake is firm around the edges, but still jiggly in the center (the jiggly area should be about the size of a quarter).

9 Remove from the oven and remove cheesecake from the water bath. Remove the foil and plastic wrap from the sides of the pan. Allow to cool at room temperature, about 40–45 minutes. Place in the refrigerator for at least 8 hours (this will help the cheesecake set completely).

10 To unmold the cheesecake, gently run a small sharp knife or small spatula around the edges of the pan. Release the latch on the side of the pan and then lift the ring straight up.

11 Slice the cheesecake into 6–8 slices and garnish each slice with a PEEPS® Candy Cane Chick.

PEEPS® Lavender Panna Cotta with Blackberry Sauce

Contributed by Chef Melanie Underwood

MAKES 4 (6-OUNCE) RAMEKINS

Ingredients

Panna Cotta

½ cup buttermilk

1 teaspoon granulated gelatin

1½ cups heavy cream

½ teaspoon dried lavender

6 PEEPS® Marshmallow Chicks or Bunnies, any color, halved

4 PEEPS® Marshmallow Chicks or Bunnies, lavender, for garnish

Blackberry Sauce

1½ cups blackberries

2 tablespoons granulated white sugar

1 tablespoon lemon juice (optional)

Directions

1 To make the panna cotta, whisk together the buttermilk and gelatin in a small bowl. Set aside.

2 In a medium saucepan, combine heavy cream, lavender, and the halved PEEPS®. Place over medium heat, whisking frequently until the PEEPS® are completely dissolved, making sure not to allow mixture to boil.

3 Remove from heat and add in the buttermilk mixture, whisking until the gelatin is completely dissolved.

4 Pour the mixture through a fine strainer to remove the lavender. Divide the mixture evenly among four 6-ounce ramekins. Chill in the refrigerator for at least 4 hours, or until firm.

5 To make the blackberry sauce, combine blackberries, sugar, and lemon juice, if using, in a medium saucepan. Cook over medium heat until berries soften, about 5 minutes. Remove from heat and allow to cool completely. Place mixture in a blender or food processor and purée until liquefied. Strain to remove any seeds.

6 To serve, run a small knife around the inside edges of a ramekin to loosen the panna cotta. Dip the bottom of the ramekin in a bowl of hot water. Place a small serving plate on top of the ramekin and immediately invert. The panna cotta should come out. If it does not, shake the ramekin back and forth to loosen and it will fall out. Repeat with remaining ramekins.

7 Garnish with a PEEPS® Chick on the side of each ramekin and drizzle over the blackberry sauce.

PEEPS® POPS AND DECORATIONS

Tie-Dye PEEPS® Bunnies

Contributed by Sugar Swings

MAKES 8-10 BUNNIES

Ingredients

1½ tablespoons meringue powder

2 cups confectioners' sugar

2½ tablespoons water

Food coloring in red, blue, green, yellow, orange, and purple

6 teaspoons clear food extract (such as lemon or vanilla), divided

12 PEEPS® Marshmallow Bunnies, any color

8–10 paper straws or lollipop sticks (optional)

6 small paintbrushes (only used for food)

Directions

1. To make royal icing, combine meringue powder, confectioners' sugar, and water in a medium bowl and beat with an electric mixer until the icing forms peaks.

2. Evenly divide the royal icing into 7 small bowls or cups. Add 1 drop of each color food coloring into each bowl, leaving one bowl of plain icing. Add 1 teaspoon extract to each bowl. Mix well with a toothpick.

3. Spread a layer of plain icing onto the front of each PEEPS® Bunny. The icing should be stiff enough that it does not spread and drip down the side of the Bunny. If icing is too thin, add more confectioners' sugar, 1 teaspoon at a time.

4. While icing is still wet, use a small paintbrush and dip into one color and paint a small dab of color in the middle of the Bunny. Use a separate brush for each color.

5. Repeat using each color, making larger and larger shapes around the original color.

6. Use a toothpick to drag through the colors from the center circle moving outward to create a tie-dye design. Drag from the original dab out to the edge of the Bunny. Repeat going around the Bunny 5–6 times.

7. Repeat for the remaining Bunnies. Change the design by changing the original placement and size of the first colored dab to alternate the tie-dye look of each Bunny.

8. Let air-dry until icing hardens, about 45 minutes, or until dry to the touch.

9. Add a paper straw or stick to make pops (optional). Insert 1 inch into Bunny.

10. Store in an airtight container at room temperature for up to 1 week.

PEEPS® Chocolate Cherry Bomb Cake Pops

Contributed by All She Cooks

MAKES 40 CAKE POPS

Ingredients

¾ cup all-purpose flour

½ cup granulated white sugar

3 tablespoons dark cocoa powder

½ teaspoon baking soda

¼ teaspoon baking powder

¼ teaspoon salt

½ cup 2% milk

3 tablespoons olive oil

1 egg

1 teaspoon vanilla extract

40 candied cherries

16 ounces white chocolate or vanilla almond bark for coating

Red decorating sugar (optional)

40 lollipop sticks

40 PEEPS® Cherries Dipped and Drizzled in Chocolate

Directions

1 In a large bowl, combine the flour, sugar, cocoa, baking soda, baking powder, and salt, and mix well.

2 In a separate large mixing bowl, combine the milk, olive oil, egg, and vanilla extract, and mix until smooth.

3 Slowly add dry ingredients to the wet ingredients and blend until the ingredients are well incorporated.

4 Using a cake pop machine, fill each cake pop reservoir with about ½ tablespoon cake batter. Top with a candied cherry, then fill on top of the cherry with another ½ tablespoon batter. To avoid a mess, you can use a plastic squeeze bottle to dispense the batter.

5 Bake each batch of cake pops for about 4–5 minutes.

6 Cool for about 10–15 minutes, then coat with melted white chocolate or almond bark and decorate with colored sugar, if desired.

7 Add a PEEPS® Cherry to each lollipop stick and then top with the Chocolate Cherry Bomb Cake Pop.

Frozen PEEPS®-icles

Contributed by A Sweet and Savory Life

MAKES 12 POPS

Ingredients

½ cup semisweet chocolate chips

¼ cup heavy cream

1 cup sprinkles

12 PEEPS® Marshmallow Bunnies, assorted colors

12 Popsicle sticks

Directions

1 Combine the chocolate chips and cream in a medium saucepan over low heat and melt until smooth. Pour into a pie plate.

2 Pour the sprinkles on a separate plate.

3 Insert a Popsicle stick in the bottom of each PEEPS® Bunny until it is halfway into the Bunny.

4 Dip the front and back of a Bunny in the chocolate, then immediately roll in the sprinkles (they will only stick to the chocolate) and place on a freezer-proof plate. Repeat with remaining Bunnies.

5 Freeze for at least 3 hours or overnight.

Push Pop PEEPS®

Contributed by Just Born

Ingredients

12 push pop containers

1 (16-ounce) container vanilla frosting

Food coloring (3 different colors are suggested)

3 quart-size zip-top storage bags (for piping frosting into push pop containers)

1 frozen pound cake, thawed (you can use miniature cupcakes or brownie bites as a substitute)

12 PEEPS® Marshmallow Bunnies, assorted colors

Sprinkles, if desired

Directions

1 Start by assembling the push pop containers, if needed.

2 Add food coloring to the frosting. If using 3 different colors, divide the frosting equally into 3 bowls and add a drop or two of color to each bowl, mixing well to combine.

3 Spoon the frosting into 3 different zip-top storage bags.

4 Place the thawed pound cake onto a cutting board and cut it in half horizontally.

5 Using a push pop container as your cutter, cut out 24 round pieces of cake. Each push pop will use 2 circles of pound cake.

6 Snip a bottom corner off each zip-top bag of frosting, leaving an approximately ¼- to ⅓-inch hole in the bottom corner of the bag.

7 Squeeze a bit of frosting into the bottom of each of your push pop containers.

8 Place a circle of pound cake into each push pop, pressing onto the top of the frosting.

9 Squeeze frosting onto the top of each of your circles of pound cake in each container; repeat with another circle of pound cake and additional frosting.

10 You can place your PEEPS® Bunnies onto your push pops whole, though they fit better if you cut them in half. Garnish with sprinkles if desired.

PEEPS® Chick Bouquet

Contributed by Making Time for Mommy

MAKES 5-6 CHICKS

Ingredients

5–6 PEEPS® Marshmallow Chicks, assorted colors

5–6 decorative straws or lollipop sticks

1 (6-ounce) package white chocolate (baking bar or chocolate chips)

Sprinkles

Clear jar

Styrofoam piece that fits in base of jar

Decorative grass, color of choice

Directions

1 Melt chocolate in the microwave for 30 seconds, then stir. Continue melting for 10-second intervals, stirring after each one, until chocolate is smooth.

2 Once melted, quickly dip the bottoms of the Chicks in the chocolate before it hardens, holding the top of the Chick with your fingers. Allow excess chocolate to drip off.

3 Gently insert lollipop sticks in the bottoms. If using straws, poke a hole into the bottom of each Chick first with a lollipop stick, then insert straw into the hole.

4 Lay pops on wax or parchment paper, add sprinkles, and chill in the refrigerator for about 30 minutes.

5 To display your bouquet, place a Styrofoam piece in the base of your clear jar and cover with decorative grass. Push the lollipop sticks or straws into the Styrofoam, varying the heights of the PEEPS® Chicks.

PEEPS® S'mores Party Pops

Contributed by Love from the Oven

MAKES 24 POPS

Ingredients

24 PEEPS® Marshmallow Bunnies, assorted colors

24 paper straws or lollipop sticks

1 (16-ounce) package chocolate almond bark or chocolate candy melts

1 cup graham cracker crumbs (about 8 sheets)

Directions

1 Line a baking sheet with a silicone baking mat or parchment paper.

2 Place a paper straw or lollipop stick halfway into each PEEPS® Bunny.

3 Melt almond bark or chocolate candy melts according to package directions.

4 Working one pop at a time, dip the top half of the PEEPS® Bunny into the melted chocolate mixture. Allow excess chocolate to drip off.

5 Working over a large bowl or plate to catch excess, sprinkle graham cracker crumbs over melted chocolate. Place pop onto baking sheet, lying flat. Repeat with remaining pops.

6 Place pops in refrigerator and allow at least 2 hours for chocolate to fully set. Store at room temperature.

Harry Potter–Inspired Bunny PEEPS®

Contributed by Sugar Swings

MAKES 3 BUNNIES

Ingredients

1 (12-ounce) package white candy melts

3 lollipop sticks

3 PEEPS® Marshmallow Bunnies, any color

1 cup chocolate chips or chocolate candy melts

½ cup orange candy melts

1 cup black candy melts

3 pieces vanilla taffy

Edible writing markers in black, blue, brown, red, and yellow

1 mini marshmallow

½ cup yellow candy melts

1 pretzel stick

Directions

1 Place white candy melts in a microwave-safe cup (deep enough to dip entire Bunny) and heat on high power in 25-second intervals until melted. Dip a lollipop stick ½-inch into the candy, then insert into the bottom of one of the PEEPS®. Let harden for 5 minutes on parchment paper. Repeat for all 3 Bunnies.

2 Holding the Bunny by the stick, dip it into the vanilla candy until coated. Tap off excess. Let harden, approximately 15 minutes at room temperature, or refrigerate for 5–10 minutes.

3 Melt chocolate chips in a quart-sized freezer bag in microwave in 15-second intervals, until just melted.

4 Snip a corner of the bag (⅛-inch) and pipe on Hermione and Harry's hair while chocolate is still melted. Use shorter lines for Harry's hair and longer lines for Hermione.

5 Repeat Steps 3 and 4 with the orange candy melts for Ron's hair.

6 Melt black candy melts in a quart-sized freezer bag in microwave in 15-second intervals, until just melted.

89

7 Snip a corner of the bag (⅛-inch) and pipe black robes on all 3 Bunnies. Use broad lines along the sides and bottom to achieve the robe look.

8 Use some of the already melted white candy to add white collars. Use a small knife or toothpick to place and spread the candy.

9 To make the ties, microwave 1 piece vanilla taffy for 5 seconds on high, or until just pliable. Roll it out flat with a rolling pin. Cut out 3 tie shapes. Use food writers to add red and yellow stripes. Alternate colors on a diagonal. Attach ties to Bunnies with a dab of melted candy and use a toothpick to position.

10 To make the scarf, microwave 1 piece vanilla taffy for 5 seconds on high, or until just pliable. Roll it out flat with a rolling pin. Cut out a long scarf shape. Use food writers to add red and yellow stripes. Alternate colors on a diagonal. Wrap around Ron Bunny and secure with a dab of melted candy. Use a toothpick to position it correctly.

11 Use a black food writer to add Harry's eyes, glasses, scar, and mouth.

12 Use a brown food writer to add Hermione's eyes and use a black food writer for her mouth.

13 Use a blue food writer to add Ron's eyes and use a black food writer for his mouth.

14 To make Hermione's book, microwave 1 piece vanilla taffy for 5 seconds on high, or until just pliable. Roll it out flat with a rolling pin. Cut out the book cover (one rectangular piece that will be folded to create the book). Flatten a mini marshmallow and insert between book cover. Use a black food writer to add the Deathly Hollows symbol. Attach to Hermione Bunny with melted candy. Use a toothpick to position it correctly.

15 To make Harry's broomstick, melt yellow candy melts in a quart-sized freezer bag in microwave in 15-second intervals, until just melted. Snip a corner of the bag (⅛-inch) and pipe broom bristles onto one end of the pretzel stick. Add the candy in long lines, going back and forth to achieve a broomstick look. Add a line of melted chocolate candy across the bristles. Let harden, about 10 minutes. Attach to Harry Bunny with melted candy. Use a toothpick to position it correctly.

16 To make Ron's wand, pipe a wand shape with some of the melted chocolate candy. Reheat as directed in Step 3 if the candy is too hard. Let harden, about 10 minutes. Attach to Ron Bunny with additional candy. Use a toothpick to position it correctly.

17 Store in airtight container at room temperature for up to 1 week.

PEEPS® Crispy Treat Pops

Contributed by Just Born

MAKES 16 POPS

Ingredients

8 PEEPS® Marshmallow Bunnies, any color

1 (16-ounce) package white candy melts

16 PEEPS® crispy rice treats (see page 31 for recipe)

Sprinkles

16 Popsicle sticks

Directions

1 Halve PEEPS® Bunnies vertically.

2 Prepare candy melts according to package instructions.

3 Using a spoon, coat one side of a crispy rice treat with the melted chocolate, then gently press a Bunny half on each side of the treat, marshmallow side down. Repeat with remaining crispy rice treats and Bunny halves.

4 Decorate the exposed chocolate with sprinkles.

5 Insert a Popsicle stick into the center bottom of each treat to create a pop.

PEEPS® S'mores Milkshake

Contributed by All She Cooks

SERVES 2

Ingredients

3 cups vanilla ice cream

1 cup milk

4 PEEPS® Chocolate Mousse Chicks Dipped in Milk Chocolate

Chocolate syrup, to taste

2 sheets graham crackers, crushed

Directions

1 In a blender, blend together ice cream, milk, and 2 PEEPS® Chicks until smooth.

2 Squeeze chocolate syrup onto the inside sides of 2 dessert glasses as decoration.

3 Add a spoonful of graham cracker crumbs to each glass.

4 Pour milkshake into glasses. Top with the remaining graham cracker crumbs, another drizzle of chocolate syrup, and a PEEPS® Chick.

Salted Caramel Marshmallow PEEPS® Dip

Contributed by Kirbie's Cravings

MAKES 4-6 SERVINGS

Ingredients

Homemade Marshmallow Fluff*

1 egg white, at room temperature

¾ cup corn syrup

¾ cup confectioners' sugar

1 teaspoon vanilla extract

Dip

12 ounces salted caramel sauce

12 PEEPS® Party Cake Chicks

3 PEEPS® Patriotic Vanilla Crème Chicks

*Or use 10 ounces store-bought marshmallow fluff

Directions

1 Preheat oven to 375°F.

2 To make the marshmallow fluff, add the egg white and corn syrup to the bowl of a stand mixer. Whip on highest speed with whisk attachment for about 5 minutes, or until mixture becomes more than double in size. Add in confectioners' sugar and vanilla extract and beat on low speed until just incorporated.

3 To make the dip, use a spatula and evenly spread marshmallow fluff across the bottom of an 8-inch skillet (or other oven-safe round pan). Evenly pour salted caramel on top of marshmallow spread.

4 Line the outer edge of the skillet with the 12 PEEPS® Party Cake Chicks, standing them upright with their faces facing outward. Place the 3 Patriotic Vanilla Crème PEEPS® in the middle, standing up and facing outward. Your skillet surface should be completely covered with PEEPS®.

5 Place in the oven and bake for about 10 minutes, or until dip is completely heated and the tops of PEEPS® have browned.

6 Serve immediately with cookies, graham crackers, or other snacks of your choice.

PEEPS® HOLIDAYS

PEEPS® Party Punch

Contributed by That's So Michelle

Ingredients

2 quarts raspberry lemonade

2 liters lemon-lime soda

4 cups or 2 pints frozen or fresh raspberries

48 ounces raspberry sherbet (optional)

30 PEEPS® Marshmallow Bunnies or Chicks, assorted colors and flavors, for floating in punch bowl and/or sticking on straws

Decorative sugar, colors of choice, for rimming glasses

24 straws (optional)

Directions

1 In a large punch bowl, mix the raspberry lemonade and lemon-lime soda. Top with raspberries and sherbet, if desired.

2 Float PEEPS® on top.

3 Serve with sugar-rimmed glasses and PEEPS® stuck on straws, if desired.

For a spring or summertime punch, try PEEPS® Sour Watermelon Chicks, PEEPS® Sweet Lemonade Chicks, or PEEPS® Blue Raspberry Chicks.

Sweetheart-Stuffed PEEPS® Treats

Contributed by Cute As a Fox

MAKES 6 TREATS

Ingredients

2 tablespoons margarine

2 cups mini marshmallows

Red gel food coloring

¼ teaspoon cherry oil flavor

3 cups crispy rice cereal

Nonstick cooking spray, for greasing

6 PEEPS® Vanilla Crème Hearts

3 pieces green licorice

2 ounces chocolate almond bark

Directions

1 In a large saucepan, melt the margarine over low heat. Add marshmallows and stir to coat. Let the marshmallows melt completely, stirring occasionally.

2 Keep the pan over low heat and add the red food coloring until the desired color is reached. Add the cherry oil flavoring and remove from heat. Pour in the rice cereal and stir until covered with the marshmallows.

3 Let the treats cool for 2–3 minutes, or until they are cool enough to handle. Spray hands with nonstick cooking spray and grab a handful of crispy treats and flatten into a circle the size of your palm. Place a PEEPS® Heart in the center and form the treats around it, covering it entirely. Add additional crispy treats to cover the Heart if needed. Repeat to make 5 additional treats. Allow the treats to cool completely on a sheet of parchment paper.

4 In a microwave-safe ramekin, heat almond bark in 30-second intervals at half power, stirring after each interval, until completely melted.

5 Drizzle the melted chocolate over each cherry, and allow the chocolate to set completely.

6 Cut a slit at the top of each treat all the way into the PEEPS® Heart. Insert a piece of green licorice for the cherry stem. To connect 2 cherries together, split the licorice with the kitchen shears, leaving 1 inch connected. For maximum freshness, prepare and serve the same day.

Sprinkled with Love PEEPS® Valentine Cookies

Contributed by Love from the Oven

Ingredients

Cookies
1 (18.25-ounce) package red velvet cake mix
2 large eggs
1 teaspoon vanilla extra
6 tablespoons butter, melted and cooled

Filling
20 PEEPS® Vanilla Crème Hearts

Frosting
1 (16-ounce) container vanilla or cream cheese frosting
Heart sprinkles (optional)

Directions

1 Preheat oven to 375°F. Line a baking sheet with parchment paper or a silicone baking mat.

2 To make the cookies, add the cake mix, eggs, vanilla extract, and cooled melted butter to a large bowl and combine until mixture comes together to form a dough.

3 Scoop up dough mixture with your hands and form forty 1-inch-round balls. Place balls on prepared baking sheet, leaving at least 2 inches between each cookie.

4 Bake for approximately 9–10 minutes, or until edges are firm. Remove from oven and allow cookies to cool on the baking sheet for approximately 5 minutes, then transfer cookies to a wire rack to cool completely, about 2 hours.

5 Once completely cooled, place cookies in freezer for 15 minutes.

6 Preheat oven to 350°F. Line a baking sheet with parchment paper or a silicone baking mat.

7 Remove cookies from freezer and place half of them (20 cookies) bottom side up on the prepared baking sheet.

8 Top each cookie with a PEEPS® Vanilla Crème Heart. Place cookies in the oven for 30–90 seconds, keeping a very close eye on the cookies (do not walk away from the oven). As soon as the Hearts start to puff up, remove the cookies from the oven.

9 Immediately and carefully (the PEEPS® will be hot!) top each cookie with a second cookie and press down gently, creating a cookie sandwich with the Heart in the center.

10 Frost with the vanilla or cream cheese frosting and garnish with sprinkles, if desired. These are best served immediately.

Uncle Sam PEEPS® Chicks

Contributed by Sugar Swings

MAKES 12 UNCLE SAMS

Ingredients

1 cup white candy melts, divided

12 mini marshmallows

¼ cup red candy melts

¼ cup blue candy melts

12 red, white, and/or blue star-shaped sprinkles

12 PEEPS® Marshmallow Chicks, blue (or try PEEPS® Patriotic Vanilla Crème Chicks or PEEPS® Blue Raspberry Chicks)

12 red, white, and/or blue circle-shaped sprinkles

24 red, white, and/or blue heart-shaped sprinkles

Directions

1 Line a baking sheet with parchment paper.

2 To make the Uncle Sam hats, place ½ cup white candy melts in a small microwave-safe bowl and melt in the microwave on high power for 20-second intervals. Stir between intervals until all candy is melted.

3 Stick a toothpick into one end of a mini marshmallow, dip marshmallow halfway into melted candy, and remove. Let harden for 10 minutes on baking sheet, candy side down. Repeat with remaining mini marshmallows.

4 Melt the red and blue candy melts in separate small microwave-safe bowls in 20-second intervals.

5 Remove toothpick from a half-dipped mini marshmallow and dip the other half into either the red or blue melted candy for the hat band. Let harden for 10 minutes on baking sheet, blue- or red-dipped side down. Repeat with remaining half-dipped marshmallows.

6 Use a toothpick or knife to scoop some of the already-melted red and blue candy onto parchment paper. Separate it into 12 pieces and spread it in a circular fashion to make it the size of a dime—these will be the bases of the hats.

7 While discs are still wet, gently press the dipped marshmallows into the center, blue- or red-dipped sides down.

8 With the already-melted red and blue candy, use a toothpick to add a small dab to the back of the star sprinkles, then gently press stars onto hat bands.

9 Melt remaining ½ cup white candy melts in a quart-size plastic freezer bag in 20-second intervals in microwave on high power for 2–3 intervals, or until all candy is melted.

10 Snip a small corner of the bag (about ⅛ inch) and pipe a dime-sized amount of candy as "hair" onto a Chick. While the hair is still wet, gently place one of the hats, with the star facing front, on top of the Chick's head. Let hair harden. Repeat with remaining Chicks.

11 Pipe more white candy onto each Chick, moving in small circular motions to resemble a curly beard.

12 Pipe a small amount of candy below beard on each Chick, then stick 2 heart-shaped sprinkles with a circle-shaped sprinkle between them for a bow tie.

13 Store in an airtight container at room temperature for up to 1 week.

PEEPS® Cats in Pumpkins

Contributed by Cute As a Fox

Ingredients

3 tablespoons margarine

10 ounces mini marshmallows

Orange gel food coloring

8 PEEPS® Chocolate Mousse Cats

6 cups crispy rice cereal

Nonstick cooking spray, for greasing

Brown licorice or pretzel sticks, cut or broken into eight 1-inch pieces

4 ounces orange candy melts

Black candy writer (optional)

Directions

1 In a large saucepan, melt the margarine over low heat. Add marshmallows and stir to coat. Let the marshmallows melt completely, stirring occasionally. Add orange food coloring until the desired color is reached. Remove from heat.

2 Pour in the rice cereal and stir until covered with marshmallow.

3 Let the treats cool for 2–3 minutes, or until they are cool enough to handle. Spray hands with nonstick cooking spray and grab a handful of crispy treats and flatten into a circle the size of your palm. Place a PEEPS® Cat in the center and tightly form a pumpkin shape around the bottom two-thirds of the Cat. Add additional crispy treats if needed to get a full, round shape. The pumpkin should be about 4 inches in diameter. Form a total of 8 pumpkins with Cats in the center and place them on a baking sheet greased with nonstick cooking spray.

4 Press the remaining crispy treats onto the greased cookie sheet in a ½-inch-thick layer.

5 Cut eight 1-inch circles for pumpkin tops from the remaining treats. Insert a piece of licorice or pretzel stick in the center of the pumpkin top to make a pumpkin stem by either cutting a slit in the pumpkin top or pressing the treats around the pumpkin stem to secure it.

6 In a microwave-safe ramekin, heat orange candy melts for 30-second intervals at half power, stirring after each interval, until completely melted.

7 Apply the melted candy to the top of a Cat head with a toothpick, then immediately press a pumpkin top onto the head. Repeat with remaining Cats and pumpkin tops. Allow the melted candy to set. To speed up the process, pop the treats in the refrigerator for 5–10 minutes.

8 If desired, add faces to the pumpkins with a black candy writer.

PEEPS® Pumpkin Patch

Contributed by Cute as a Fox

MAKES 1 PUMPKIN PATCH

Ingredients

Base

3 tablespoons margarine

10 ounces mini marshmallows

6 cups chocolate-flavored crispy rice cereal

Nonstick cooking spray, for greasing

24 PEEPS® Marshmallow Pumpkins

¼ cup orange sanding sugar

Decorating Items (optional)

2 ounces yellow licorice string

3 sheets graham crackers

Black food writer

1 pretzel stick

4 ounces chocolate almond bark

1 tablespoon green fondant

Directions

1 To create the base, in a large saucepan, heat margarine over low heat. When the margarine has melted, add marshmallows. Heat marshmallows until completely melted, stirring occasionally. Remove from heat.

2 Stir in the chocolate-flavored crispy rice cereal until cereal is completely covered in marshmallow. Pour mixture onto a baking sheet greased with nonstick cooking spray.

3 Spray hands with nonstick cooking spray and press the treats down into a 10 x 10-inch square. Let the treats set at room temperature, about 30 minutes.

4 With a serrated knife, cut a 4 x 10-inch section of treats from the square. Further divide that 4 x 10-inch section into a 2½ x 10-inch and 1½ x 10-inch section. Stack the cut portions onto the larger base piece to create a tiered stand for the PEEPS® Pumpkins. Before decorating, transfer the base to the serving platter.

5 Using a sharp knife, carefully separate the PEEPS® Pumpkins from one another. (For easier cutting, dip the knife in hot water and then dry before cutting Pumpkins.) Press the cut sides and tops, with the exposed marshmallow, into orange sanding sugar to camouflage cut edges. Leave any cut Pumpkin bottoms white. The exposed marshmallow will help the Pumpkins adhere to the crispy rice base.

6 Start adding PEEPS® Pumpkins to the crispy rice base.

7 Let your creative side take over here! Here are some additional decorating ideas for the pumpkin patch:

- Create "hay bundles" with yellow licorice string.
- Make a pumpkin sign by writing on graham cracker with a food writer. Attach the sign to a pretzel stick with melted chocolate almond bark.
- Add stems and leaves to some pumpkins with green fondant and pretzel sticks.
- Create a pumpkin bin by pressing graham crackers into the crispy rice base. Add yellow licorice string for hay. For added stability, use melted chocolate almond bark to glue the graham crackers together.

Pumpkin Cream Pie with Turkey PEEPS®

Contributed by A Sweet and Savory Life

MAKES 8-12 SERVINGS
(THIS RECIPE REQUIRES
OVERNIGHT REFRIGERATION)

Ingredients

Crust

6 tablespoons butter, melted

1½ cups graham cracker crumbs (about 12 sheets)

¼ cup granulated white sugar

Filling

8 ounces cream cheese, at room temperature

4 tablespoons butter, at room temperature

1½ cups granulated white sugar

1 tablespoon vanilla extract

1 (15-ounce) can pumpkin purée (not pumpkin pie filling)

1 teaspoon pumpkin pie spice mix

1 cup heavy cream

2 tablespoons maple syrup

2 tablespoons confectioners' sugar

Turkey PEEPS®

15 toothpicks

6 PEEPS® Orange Chicks Dipped in Milk Chocolate

30 candy corns (approximately)

Shaved chocolate, for garnish

Directions

1 To make the crust, combine the melted butter, graham cracker crumbs, and sugar in a large bowl until evenly blended. Pat the mixture firmly into an ungreased 9-inch pie plate and refrigerate at least 20 minutes.

2 To make the pumpkin filling, place the cream cheese and butter in a large bowl and beat with an electric mixer until very smooth. Beat in the sugar and vanilla extract. When it is fully incorporated, add the pumpkin purée and pumpkin pie spice mix. Spoon into the prepared crust and refrigerate overnight until firm.

 110

3 Using an electric mixer, whip the cream to soft peaks. Add the maple syrup and confectioners' sugar and whip to stiff peaks. Spread over the chilled pumpkin mixture and refrigerate until serving (may be done up to 6 hours in advance).

4 To make the turkey PEEPS®, cut 12 toothpicks in half. Insert each half through the white end of a candy corn, leaving about half the length of the toothpick exposed. If the candy corn breaks, warm it in the microwave for a few seconds to make it more pliable.

5 Insert 4 candy corns into the back neck of each PEEPS® Chick to form the turkey feathers. Push until the toothpick no longer shows.

6 Cut the yellow ends from several candy corns in a wedge shape to form beaks, and mold the orange into a dangling globular shape to form wattles. Halve 3 more toothpicks and insert each half through a beak and wattle, leaving a little toothpick exposed. Attach to the PEEPS® Chicks with the exposed toothpick.

7 To serve, sprinkle the shaved chocolate lightly over the whipped cream topping and place the 6 turkey PEEPS® on the pie.

Christmas PEEPS® Peppermint Pudding Pie

Contributed by Just Born

Ingredients

1 (3.9-ounce) package instant chocolate pudding

1½ cups cold milk

½ teaspoon peppermint extract

2 cups whipped topping, divided

1 premade chocolate piecrust

Chocolate syrup

Candy canes, crushed

8 PEEPS® Candy Cane Chicks Dipped in Chocolate

Directions

1 Beat pudding mix, milk, and peppermint extract with a whisk for 2 minutes.

2 Fold 1 cup whipped topping into pudding mixture.

3 Spoon mixture into piecrust. Place in refrigerator for at least 1 hour.

4 Top with remaining 1 cup whipped topping.

5 Chill for at least 3 hours prior to serving.

6 When serving, garnish each slice of pie with chocolate sauce and crushed candy cane, and top with a PEEPS® Candy Cane Chick Dipped in Chocolate.

Gingerbread PEEPS®
Hot Chocolate

Contributed by Kirbie's Cravings

Ingredients

Whipped Cream

½ cup heavy cream

1 tablespoon granulated white sugar

Hot Chocolate

¼ cup water

1½ cups lowfat milk

2 tablespoons unsweetened cocoa powder

2 tablespoons granulated white sugar

½ ounce chopped dark chocolate

4 PEEPS® Gingerbread Men,
plus additional 2 PEEPS® Gingerbread Men
or PEEPS® Chocolate Mousse Reindeer, for
topping hot chocolate (optional)

Directions

1 To make the whipped cream, add cream and sugar to bowl of stand mixer. Mix on highest speed with whisk attachment until stiff peaks form. Refreigerate until using.

2 To make the hot chocolate, add water, milk, cocoa, sugar, and chocolate to a small saucepan. Over low heat, stir constantly until chocolate is completely melted and uniform in color.

3 Add in 4 PEEPS® Gingerbread Men, stirring until completely dissolved.

4 Evenly pour hot chocolate into 2 mugs. Top each with a PEEPS® Gingerbread Man or Chocolate Mousse Reindeer, if desired. Serve while hot.

PEEPS® Gingerbread House

Contributed by Cute As a Fox

Ingredients

1 gingerbread house (store-bought or homemade)

Tile Roof

Approximately 100 candy discs
Royal icing (store-bought or homemade)

Wreath

1 green gummy ring
Red licorice string, 5 inches long
Royal icing (store-bought or homemade)

Door

1 sheet graham cracker
Red fondant
Fondant imprint mat (optional)
1 small candy-coated chocolate
Royal icing (store-bought or homemade)
1 PEEPS® Gingerbread Man

Christmas Light Strand

Green licorice string
Christmas light sprinkles
Green royal icing (store-bought or homemade)

Christmas Trees

6 PEEPS® Christmas Trees
6 mini pretzel sticks

Bundled-Up Gingerbread Men

3 pieces red fruit leather (1 x 4 inches each)
6 PEEPS® Gingerbread Men
6 red MIKE AND IKE® Brand candies
2 ounces red candy melts
Toothpick

Santas

4 ounces red candy melts
Toothpick
6 conical corn chips
2 ounces white almond bark
6 PEEPS® Gingerbread Men

Snowmen

4 ounces chocolate almond bark
8 PEEPS® Marshmallow Snowmen
Snowflake sprinkles
2 toothpicks
3 orange MIKE AND IKE® Brand candies
2 ounces white chocolate almond bark
Candy pearls, or other small, white, round candies
Snowflake sprinkles

Peppermint Sleds

4 ounces red candy melts

3 graham cracker sheets

6 mini candy canes

3 PEEPS® Candy Cane Chicks Dipped in Chocolate

Directions

1 To make the tile roof, pipe a row of royal icing, starting at the bottom edge of one side of the roof, then gently press the candy discs into the icing, placing them in a straight row right next to each other. Next, pipe a row of icing directly above the first row. Cut a disc in half and press it into the icing with the cut edge facing the front of the house—this will help stagger the rows of candy tiles. Place whole candy discs down overlapping half of the first row. Repeat these steps until the entire roof is covered. Every other row of candy should begin with a halved candy disc. To finish the top of the roof, pipe a line of royal icing at the apex of the roof and lay a row of tiles parallel to the ground.

2 To make the wreath, tie the smallest bow possible with the red licorice string. Trim the ends of the licorice to the desired length. Adhere the bow to the green gummy ring with a dab of royal icing. Attach the wreath to the gingerbread house also using royal icing.

3 To make the door, wrap a graham cracker sheet in a damp paper towel and microwave for 10–20 seconds, until the graham cracker is slightly soft. Roll out a small amount of red fondant, enough to cover the graham cracker, to ⅛ inch thick with a rolling pin. Place the fondant on the graham cracker, covering it completely. If you want added texture, press a fondant imprint mat onto the fondant, then peel back the mat.

Secure a candy-coated chocolate onto the fondant as a doorknob with a small dot of royal icing. Use royal icing to glue the door into place in a partially open position, then place a PEEPS® Gingerbread Man just inside the door, with his head peeking out.

4 To make the Christmas light strand, measure the pitch of the roof of the house and cut a piece of green licorice string to that length. Lay the licorice string on a sheet of parchment paper and use green royal icing to adhere a Christmas light sprinkle to the licorice string every ½ inch. Allow the royal icing to harden at least 30 minutes before moving the light string. Use dots of green royal icing to apply the light string to the gingerbread house.

5 To make the Christmas trees, use a sharp knife to poke a hole in the bottom of each of the PEEPS® Christmas Trees, then firmly insert a pretzel stick into the bottom of each Tree. To create visual interest and variety, vary the heights of the Trees by breaking the pretzel sticks into different lengths before inserting into the PEEPS®.

6 To make the bundled-up Gingerbread Men, use kitchen shears to halve the fruit leather lengthwise, for a total of 6 strips. Wrap the fruit strips around the necks of the PEEPS® Gingerbread Men as scarves. Next, cut the rounded ends off each of the red MIKE AND IKE® candies to create the earmuff pads. Heat the red candy melts in a microwave-safe ramekin for 15-second intervals at half power, stirring after each interval, until completely melted. Using a toothpick, place a small amount of melted candy on each side of the Gingerbread Men's heads and press the cut MIKE AND IKE® candies in place. Hold in place approximately 30 seconds, or until the candy is adhered to the PEEPS®. Now, dip a toothpick in the melted red candy and draw a line of candy across the top of each of the Gingerbread

Men's heads, connecting the earmuff pads. Allow the melted candy to set approximately 15 minutes, or until the candy changes from glossy to matte in appearance.

7 To make the Santas, heat red candy melts in a microwave-safe ramekin for 30-second intervals at half power, stirring after each interval, until completely melted. Insert a toothpick into the end of a conicle corn chip and dip it into the melted candy. Gently tap the toothpick to remove any excess candy. Carefully remove the corn chip from the toothpick and allow to set in a standing position on a sheet of parchment paper, about 10 minutes. Repeat for remaining corn chips. Next, heat white almond bark in a microwave-safe ramekin for 15-second intervals at half power, stirring after each interval, until completely melted. Dip both ends of each chip into the white almond bark to create the white trim. Return the hats to the parchment paper and allow to set completely. To speed up the process, refrigerate the Santa hats for 5–10 minutes. Once set, use a toothpick to apply a small amount of melted white almond bark to the top of the PEEPS® Gingerbread Men's heads. Place a Santa hat on top of each head and allow the almond bark to set.

8 To make the Snowmen, heat chocolate almond bark in a microwave-safe ramekin for 30-second intervals at half power, stirring after each interval, until completely melted. Dip the hat portion of each of the PEEPS® Snowmen into the melted chocolate. Gently shake off any excess chocolate. Place the Snowmen on a baking sheet or parchment paper, plain side up. While the chocolate is still wet, decorate the hat with snowflake sprinkles. Next, dip the end of a toothpick into the chocolate and draw eyes and a mouth on the snowman. Make sure to leave room for a candy nose. Cut the orange MIKE AND IKE® candies in half. Cut the halves into half again horizontally. Heat the white chocolate almond bark in a microwave-safe ramekin for 15-second

intervals at half power, stirring after each interval, until completely melted. Use a toothpick to apply a small amount of white chocolate to the candy nose and place one on each Snowman's face. Apply candy pearl "buttons" to the Snowmen, using the melted white chocolate as adhesive. Allow the Snowmen to set in a horizontal position, approximately 15 minutes, or until the candy bark has changed from glossy to matte in appearance.

9 To make the peppermint sleds, heat red candy melts in a microwave-safe ramekin for 30-second intervals at half power, stirring after each interval, until completely melted. Dip one side of each graham cracker sheet in the candy melts. If necessary, use a spoon to spread the melted candy around and make sure the edges are coated as well. Gently shake off any excess candy. Place the coated graham crackers on a baking sheet or parchment paper. While the candy is still wet, place a mini candy cane (sled runner) on each side of the sleds. The melted candy will set and keep them in place. Finally, place a PEEPS® Candy Cane Chick in the center of each sled while the candy is still wet. Allow the sled to set approximately 15 minutes, or until the candy has changed from glossy to matte in appearance.

PEEPS® Red Velvet Holiday Cupcakes

Contributed by All She Cooks

MAKES 24 CUPCAKES

Ingredients

Cupcakes

2½ cups all-purpose flour

2 tablespoons dark cocoa powder

½ teaspoon baking soda

2 teaspoons baking powder

1 teaspoon salt

1 cup or 2 sticks unsalted butter, at room temperature

2 cups granulated white sugar

3 eggs, at room temperature

2 tablespoons red food coloring

1½ tablespoons water

2 teaspoons vanilla extract

1 cup milk

Chocolate Red Velvet Ganache

1 cup heavy cream

1 cup semisweet chocolate chips

3 PEEPS® Red Velvet Chicks Dipped in Cream Fudge

Buttercream Frosting

1 cup or 2 sticks unsalted butter, at room temperature

6 cups confectioners' sugar

2 teaspoons vanilla extract

3½ tablespoons milk, divided

Directions

1 Preheat oven to 350°F. Line two 12-count cupcake pans with cupcake liners or grease and flour pans.

2 To make the cupcakes, combine the flour, cocoa, baking soda, baking powder, and salt in a large mixing bowl, and mix well.

3 In separate large mixing bowl, beat butter with electric mixer until smooth. Add in sugar and mix until well blended. Continue mixing while adding eggs, food coloring, water, and vanilla extract.

4 Slowly add in dry ingredients, making sure the batter is well incorporated. Finally, slowly mix in the milk until smooth.

5 Pour batter into a gallon-size zip-top plastic bag and cut off one corner of the bag, making a pea-sized opening. Use that to neatly squeeze batter into each cupcake liner, making sure each liner is three-quarters full. Bake for 25–27 minutes, inserting a toothpick to check for doneness. Toothpick should come out clean.

6 Remove from the oven and let cool, about 20–30 minutes. Use a cupcake corer to remove a small area inside each cupcake for the filling.

7 To make the ganache, bring cream to a boil in a small saucepan over medium heat while stirring constantly. Add in chocolate chips and stir until smooth. Remove from heat and place saucepan in refrigerator until cooled, about 20 minutes.

8 Place metal mixing bowl and whisk attachment into the refrigerator to chill, about 15–20 minutes.

9 Once chocolate ganache has chilled, pour into chilled mixing bowl and whip for 4–5 minutes on high speed.

10 Roughly chop PEEPS® Red Velvet Chicks into small pieces. Stir into thickened, whipped chocolate ganache.

11 Pour ganache into gallon-size zip-top plastic bag and snip off a corner in order to neatly pipe into cupcakes.

12 To make the buttercream frosting, blend butter in mixer until smooth. Add in confectioners' sugar and mix until well combined. Add in vanilla extract and 2 tablespoons milk. Mix together until smooth. Continue adding milk, 1 tablespoon at a time, until frosting reaches desired thickness.

13 Scoop frosting into either a piping bag with a decorative frosting tip, or cut the corner off of a gallon-sized zip-top plastic bag, as done with the ganache in Step 11. Pipe frosting onto the cupcake starting at the outer edge and moving around the top of the cupcake in a circular movement toward the center. Squeeze a little extra frosting out on the center of the cupcake and pull up on the piping (or zip-top) bag to give a more decorative finish to the cupcake.

PEEPS® Birthday Cinnamon Rolls

Contributed by Love from the Oven

Ingredients

Rolls

¾ cup 2% or whole milk

¼ cup or ½ stick butter

3½ cups all-purpose flour, divided, plus additional for dusting

1 (0.25 ounce) packet rapid rise yeast

½ teaspoon salt

¼ cup granulated white sugar

¼ cup very warm water

1 egg

Cinnamon Mixture

¼ cup or ½ stick butter, softened

¾ cup granulated white sugar

¾ cup brown sugar, packed

2 tablespoons ground cinnamon

2 teaspoons cornstarch

Frosting and Topping

4 ounces cream cheese, softened

¼ cup or ½ stick butter, softened

1 teaspoon vanilla extract

1 tablespoon 2% or whole milk

1½ cups confectioners' sugar

¼ teaspoon salt

1 tablespoon butter

4 PEEPS® Party Cake Chicks

Sprinkles, for garnish

12 PEEPS® Marshmallow Chicks, assorted colors, for garnish

Directions

1 To make the rolls, heat milk and butter in a saucepan until butter melts and mixture starts to bubble. Remove from heat and let cool to lukewarm, about 20 minutes.

2 In a large bowl, add 2½ cups flour, yeast, salt, and sugar, and combine well.

123

3 Add warm milk mixture and warm water to flour mixture and stir to begin to combine. Add in egg and mix well. Add in remaining 1 cup of flour a little at a time until well combined.

4 Once dough has combined, knead well for 3–5 minutes. If dough is still sticky, add more flour, 1 spoonful at a time. The dough should be easy to work with and not overly sticky.

5 Lightly oil or butter a large bowl. Place dough in the bowl and cover the top of the bowl with a damp cloth. Place in a warm, draft-free spot for approximately 15 minutes.

6 Remove dough from the bowl and roll out on a floured surface into a rectangle approximately 12 x 9 inches in size.

7 To make the cinnamon mixture, spread softened butter over surface of the dough. Sprinkle with a mixture of the ¾ cup white sugar, brown sugar, cinnamon, and cornstarch. Roll dough up into a log, starting with one of the longer edges and pinch seam to seal.

8 Using a knife, cut dough into 12 equal pieces. Lightly brush a 13 x 9-inch pan with butter and place dough pieces in the pan. Cover and let rise at least 30 minutes (60 minutes is ideal if time allows).

9 Preheat oven to 350°F. Bake rolls for approximately 17–20 minutes, or until lightly browned. Remove from the oven. You will need to spread with frosting immediately.

10 To make the frosting, beat cream cheese and ¼ cup (½ stick) softened butter with a mixer until creamy. Add in vanilla extract and milk, and mix until well combined. Slowly add in confectioners' sugar and salt, and beat until fluffy. Set aside.

11 In a heavy saucepan on low heat, melt 1 tablespoon butter with PEEPS® Party Cake Chicks. Stir until PEEPS® have dissolved and combined with melted butter. Remove from heat and allow to cool for approximately 5 minutes.

12 Add PEEPS® mixture to frosting and mix with an electric mixer until well combined. If the frosting is too thin, add extra confectioners' sugar, 1 tablespoon at a time, until desired consistency is reached.

13 Spread frosting onto cinnamon rolls while they are still hot, allowing frosting to melt into the cinnamon rolls. Immediately add sprinkles. Top each cinnamon roll with a PEEPS® Chick and serve.

About the Contributors
(and Fellow PEEPS® Lovers)

Sally McKenney of *Sally's Baking Addiction*

Sally McKenney is the creator of the hugely popular blog *Sally's Baking Addiction* (sallysbakingaddiction.com), which regularly receives over five million visitors a month, and she is the author of *Sally's Baking Addiction* and *Sally's Candy Addiction*. She has been featured on the Huffington Post and in *Redbook*, *Country Living*, and more. Sally currently lives in Philadelphia, Pennsylvania, with her husband, Kevin, and their rescue German shepherd/rottweiler mix, Jude.

Christi Johnstone of *Love from the Oven*

Christi Johnstone is the blogger, baker, and photographer behind the yummy food blog *Love from the Oven* (lovefromtheoven.com), which receives well over a half million visitors a month. She has appeared on national TV and is the author of *Smart Cookie: Transform Store-Bought Cookies into Amazing Treats*. Christi currently lives in Phoenix, Arizona, with her husband and two daughters.

Jennifer Lee of *Kirbie's Cravings*

Jennifer Lee is the creator of the popular San Diego–based food blog *Kirbie's Cravings* (kirbiecravings.com), which boasts over a million visitors a month. Jennifer's recipes have been featured on the Huffington Post, BuzzFeed, Fox News, and the Food Network, and in *Cosmopolitan* and *Saveur* magazines. She is the author of *5-Minute Mug Cakes* and the upcoming *Clean & Easy Dump Cakes*.

Alicia Peiffer of *Making Time for Mommy*

Alicia Peiffer is a Chicago-area mom of two active, sports-loving little boys. She started her blog, *Making Time for Mommy* (makingtimeformommy.com), in 2008, which was ranked as one of the Top 100 Most Influential Parenting blogs in 2015. Alicia was also ranked by Cision as a Top 50 U.S. Mom Blogger. She has been featured in *M Magazine* and on the Huffington Post, Disney's Spoonful, and more.

Chef Melanie Underwood at *Melanieunderwood.com*

Chef Melanie Underwood is a celebrated pastry chef who has worked at the Four Seasons Hotel, the Plaza Hotel, and Torre di Pisa in New York City. She has been sharing her expertise as a cooking and baking instructor for the Institute of Culinary Education since 1996, and she tests and develops recipes for corporate clients. Melanie has been seen on national TV, including the *Today Show*, *Live with Regis and Kelly*, CNN, and the Food Network. She has also been featured in the *New York Times*, the *New York Daily News*, *Fine Cooking Magazine*, and more.

Ashley Fox Whipple of *Cute As a Fox*

Ashley Fox Whipple is the creator of the blog *Cute As a Fox* (cuteasafox.com), and her edible food creations have been spotted in *Parade* magazine and on Foodgawker, Craftgawker, TasteSpotting, and more. She is the author of *Super Cute Crispy Treats*, and she lives in Phoenix, Arizona, with her family.

Marge Perry of *A Sweet and Savory Life*

An award-winning food writer, Marge Perry's work appears regularly in many top magazines, including *EveryDay with Rachael Ray*, *Allrecipes*, *Self*, and others. She teaches cooking at the Institute of Culinary Education and food writing at New York University, where she often gives PEEPS®-related assignments to her students. Her next cookbook, written with her recipe-developer husband, David Bonom, comes out in 2017. Follow her life at the stove, around the table, and on the road at her blog, *A Sweet and Savory Life* (asweetandsavorylife.com), where you'll also find hundreds of recipes and pretty pictures.

Michelle Cordero of *That's So Michelle*

Michelle Cordero is a food and lifestyle blogger who loves to entertain. Her blog, *That's So Michelle* (thatssomichelle.com), features incredible party creations that have been featured on BuzzFeed and in *Bon Appétit*, *Cosmopolitan*, *Glamour*, *Country Living*, *Redbook*, and more. She is the author of *Jelly Shots: A Rainbow of 70 Boozy Recipes*. Michelle is a former reporter who has appeared on Fox News and MSNBC, and she now works in Washington, DC, in media relations. She lives in Virginia with her husband, son, and yellow lab.

Michelle Clausen of *Sugar Swings! Serve Some*

Michelle Clausen is the owner, writer, and edible treat creator behind the blog *Sugar Swings! Serve Some* (sugarswings.com). You'll find delicious, sugar-inspired treats on her site with a lot of geek and pop culture sprinkled in. Michelle—a pharmacist by trade—loves to create unique and fun treats for her three kids and for busy parents like herself. Sometimes she'll also sneak in a healthy dessert, too (well, relatively healthy). Michelle can be found on most social media accounts as @sugarswings so swing by and say "hi"!

Jessica McCoy of *All She Cooks*

Jessica McCoy is the food photographer, recipe developer, food stylist, and blogger behind *All She Cooks* (allshecooks.com). She loves creating fun and easy recipes and meal plans for thousands of fans, and she believes in simplicity so that we can fit delicious food into our busy schedules.

About Just Born, Inc.

Just Born, Inc. is a family-owned candy manufacturer that has been in business since 1923. Just Born is the manufacturer of PEEPS®, MIKE AND IKE®, HOT TAMALES®, GOLDENBERG'S® PEANUT CHEWS®, TEENEE BEANEE® Brand Gourmet Jelly Beans, and JUST BORN® Brand Jelly Beans. Their corporate headquarters are located in Bethlehem, Pennsylvania.

Just Born acquired the Rodda Candy Company of Lancaster, PA, in 1953. As a result of the acquisition, the PEEPS® Chick was "hatched"! What once took 27 hours to make by hand with a pastry tube was cut down to a 6-minute process through mechanization created by Bob Born, son of founder Sam Born. On average, more than 5 million PEEPS® marshmallow confections are made every day in the USA.

For over 60 years, PEEPS® has traditionally been an iconic brand found in Easter baskets everywhere. Today, PEEPS® Brand marshmallow can be found in a variety of colors, shapes, flavors, and sizes. You can get PEEPS® for all of your favorite seasons, including Easter, Halloween, Christmas, Valentine's Day, and Summer. Whether you are looking for great shapes to decorate or bake with, or are looking for amazing seasonal flavors to bite into, there is a PEEPS® product for you! And, because there are so many fans, PEEPS® has its own merchandise line, which is marketed through PEEPS & COMPANY®.

For product information, please visit www.marshmallowpeeps.com.

For retail merchandise, please visit www.peepsandcompany.com.